UTTERANCE OF A CAGE GIRL

LEENA AFSHA ISHROT

ISBN 979-888591489-5

To those, who can relates these poems
You're growing...
You will definitely find a way to fly
Be patient
Mark the timing of your life
Cause Almighty never puts in a situation
In which you can't get through

Contents

Contents

Acknowledgements

I would like to show gratitude foremost to the Lord, who showers unending grace upon me. Today wherever I stand, it is all because of my family and of their love and support. Besides them, I'm blessed for having good friends viz., Esther C. Douglas, Sneha Paul, Priya Deb, Monalisa Das and Salim Rahmani, who hold a special place in my life. They're like a torchbearer in my life. They have pointed out my errors and helped me to mould to become my best version.

About The Author

Leena AfshaI Ishrot

Graduated in English literature and currently, a student of law, Leena Afsha Ishrot, is a 21-year-old young aspiring poet. Her works are-

"Poetry is all about emotions", "कुछ नज़्म प्यार के"।

These are two solo poetry books of hers. Other than these, she has compiled two anthologies, namely -

"Ephemeral" and "Walking on Broken Heels".

Her various poetries have been published in numerous

anthologies.

You can contact her:
Instagram: **@Poetry_an_undying_emotion**
Twitter: @**AfshaLeena**
Email id: **leenasfsha@gmail.com**

About The Book

In this book, the poet depicts the gush of emotions and about why thoughts matter. In a day, an individual goes through many ebb and flow, but the poet had picked up some moments to share with you all.

She presented about a girl who's caged and needs a way to unlock the cage. A girl who wants to climb the stairs to taste success. Sometimes it becomes too heavy to bottle up things within an individual, therefore as a medium, she chose to jot down in paper in a proper way with appropriate diction.

CHAPTER ONE

Can I live for myself?

I want to take a lonely ride
Where there resides a little tranquility*
I want to breathe under a blue sky, amidst nature
Where there is none except me and twinkle star
Where I can scream on top so that my lungs explode
But,
Why do I have to hide what I feel?
Why do I have to tolerate comments about my skin?
Why do I have to sacrifice my dreams for the sake of others?
If Lord has made me without discrimination
Why do people around me set limits?
It's because I was born as a girl!
As if we are bound to live within four walls of our home,
Not every girl has born to cook
Some are living their dream job too;
A girl is like a bird,
Wings are attached to fly and not to tie.

CHAPTER TWO

When shall I return?

Is what each one queries
Do they want to know, am I living?
Heal- it sounds so ridiculous (to them)
No more their words affect me
Minutely they differentiate between my brother and me
Not every time I need relationship hashtags
Sometimes I need a space to live on my own price tag

When shall I return?
Anything which is not straight, according to them is meaningless in life
Do they want to know behind the scenes, why I separate myself from the crew?
I am jolly far away
Why do I need to always depend upon my father or my future spouse?
Ain't capable of taking care of my own?
Ain't capable of taking care of my livelihood?

When shall I return?
Is what each one queries
I hang myself every day in the dusk
To wake up with stains of ropes on my neck

But seldom does anyone notices
They just need my physical presence
Hardly matter whether I am a-lived or dead

CHAPTER THREE

Does love mean to be caged?

I am a caged bird,
I longed to fly high in the open sky,
Where there are no shackles of discussions,
Where my wings aren't cut short,
Cause I want to fly high in the open sky,
Leaning near the windowpane,
I wonder how a free bird roams!

My soul is unrestricted
But my body is bandaged with people's statements
For doing what's not right according to few

For me, homecoming is depressing
Independent is what I need in real
But in reality, I am enveloped by limitations
Dreams of a free bird vary from caged birds,

All I fancy is solitude
But I bound to do what's caused me fear
I can inhale and exhale in crew,
Yet I feel suffocation in a crowd.

Love is not all about cuddle
But to live freely as they yearn.

I ain't a doll wherever and whoever wants to do on and off with my existence
I am a leader of my journey
Who can make her rhythms.

CHAPTER FOUR

A girl with dreams

i.
I want to be a singer
So that people can relate and sing in the loop.

ii.
I want to be a doctor
To heal people around me but I end up healing myself.

iii.
I want to practice law
But when I said- I will sue my dad for hitting repeatedly in the back portion of my head
Then my mother replied: "will you disclose your father? What kinda kid you are? This is what we taught you!"

iv.
But
I end up writing vigorously
It's not easy to remain silent
And to make things that never happened.

v.
Mixing a bowl of bitter words, aggression, frustration

To develop a descant attitude, walking, and speaking skills
But
If you speak out in wrath - they'll remember you as sin maker.

vi.
I choose to write because
My nib of the pen knows the value of tears
As NO ONE cares what I am going through
But in the end, they will remember me - as either lived a worth living life or wasted her life.

vii.
She is a girl, she is born to cook
I believe- I ain't born to feed my only family
I was born to feed the starving, budding artists who waited for spring to bloom;
As because they are starving, they're not meant to have a family soon!

viii.
Heartbreak is not the end of my life
I have born to face the challenges on my journey

CHAPTER FIVE

The "happy" game

Adjacent to the door of my destination
But happiness is playing hide and seek
I lost myself, my companion in this journey.
There are a few who applauded my performances
I feel strange to catch a glimpse of
It is surely not easy to fall and break
And not to lean like Pisa* but to stand high
By polishing heart
By wearing a humanitarian jacket.

Poet waters dead plants

Poets have the power to turn yellow leaves into greenly
By using imagery*, metaphor", and symbolism*.

CHAPTER SIX

Thoughts matter...

I introduce myself as
Who goes down momentarily to ink sensations
But the law subject to statements over emotions

Nor my father's father or his father
Know how thoughts matter
But I was born to glow in the light

I was born to carve my path
With the effort of the wisdom
Which I gain from my experience

CHAPTER SEVEN

She is both fire and ice

She had been through hell
But people see her as a cruel
But none had seen her demons
She conquered them
She had marks on her hands, thighs, legs and in clitoris
She had been a silent victim of violent mental disturbance

She hardly show her bright side
As if they bought her to use a carnal* tool
They dug her to dumped

But someone she managed to flee
To save her life

Rightly placed

I belong to twilight sparkle and hazy mornings

CHAPTER EIGHT

I'm at my best state, when I am with myself

Am I crazy?
Am I mysterious?
Am I too complex?
Do I have a tag of my own?
Or alike as egoist
Is suffering perpetual?
Who am I?

Just a girl who ink emotions
I lose myself
I dream, I weave, I sink
When I am with myself, I am living
When I am with myself, I dream
When I am with myself, I live without chains
When I am with myself, I absorbed lights

I feel sorry for myself, sometimes
I feel sorry for not living, I want to
I feel sorry for myself for lying to myself when I wear fake smile
I feel sorry for myself, when I taste sourness

I feel sorry for myself when I procrastinate
I feel sorry for myself, when I fail to keep my promise
I feel sorry for myself, for walking on the graveyard

CHAPTER NINE

If I ain't a poet, who am I?

I am no less than an owl
To sleep in the night
Doesn't fit in my cup.

The beauty of night enhance me to work
With a handful of (in) appropriate words
In a (un) organized manner.

Attracts by the purity of moon
Speaks to fireflies under a starry night
Nonetheless less adorable to darkness.

Time flies
A tight hug with unhappiness
Flows my words in solitude.

World taught to hide distress
Behind broad smiles
Where each one succumbed to different tragedies.

Love,

Tranquility of mind
With a right partner

Success and failure
Two sides of the same coin
Patience is the ingredient.

War inside me
Keeps me alive
The day it will end, I will be a dust.

Bleeding reddish and blue poetries
Unknowingly mould as an alien to others
Finding peace by fantasizing thoughts.

The poet in me buries
I often wonder to Muse
Why does it fail to inspire me, these days?

Like a heavy downpour
Will my words come back to me?
As it used to do.

I've forgotten how to jot down
Giving space for my betterment
But life is moving in an anti-clockwise direction

What if words scream!

Wearing a mask of miseries
Shrieking with a shivering throat of poverty
Sinking wordage in the edges to alive

CHAPTER TEN

Serenity is in art

Breathing poetries
Stitching zentangle patterns
Gulping red hot salty tears
Dwelling in the bottom of the heart
Smiling with heavy hearts
Creating mandala for peace of mind
Painting aura of sanguine* sky

CHAPTER ELEVEN

ABCD...

Attached with raw genres
Blinded by jaggery words
Constant procrastination
Declutter bundles of yellow pages
Eyes on the soil
Fake smile, fake promise, frankly speaking
Grudges of past remorse
Hundreds of sleepless nights
Impulsive acts drained off
Jumbled life
Kaleidoscope of shattered universe
Longing to be elated me
Moksha
Niche with underrated value
Odyssey
Plucking innocent lives
Quintessentially subject to carnal* desires
Rush in my mind
Sacrifice, sober, self - approach
Taurus bleeding on typewriter machine
"Us" - seems sarcastic
VIBGYOR, sour days
Welcome to world full of barter and less of love

Young and lively spirit
Zeal to overcome obstacles.

CHAPTER TWELVE

It's totally okay to feel you are not okay!

Somedays I feel empty. I feel nothing. It's not easy to smile with a soaking voice. It's not easy to
remain practical everytime. It's not easy to hold heavy for long. It's not easy to keep isolated
from all. Few are empty and sensitive. Sometimes I feel like screaming aloud, to feel tranquility.
But I failed to do so. I am with my burning ashes due to which I am anguished at times and on
the other I am calm. I am not in search of the answer "why me?" Rather I am grateful for going
left and walking in the woods to polish my life with scars. This suffering, this torment is the only
house of my sorrow, abode of heart lies here. The more the get attached, the more agony of life,
I could sense. The storm outside is less powerful than the inner storms of mine. These days
nothing excites me. As if I am longing for freedom from the external world.

CHAPTER THIRTEEN

Lost lake

Is that so easy as the title holds?

Floating like a corpse*
Sometimes it feels too heavy to take a breath
But there is barely alternate option:
Other than inhaling and exhale

Do you know divorce is beautiful?
Like a bird free from restraint
Who always want to fly high
No matter to catch her prey,
She needs to look beneath
But again she flies above.

Do you know heartbroken people are beautiful?
With a fragmentize heart,
They weave hope
They become realistic
They bottle up many emotions within themselves
Only to overcome ghosts of the past.

Do you know everything seems to be precisely accurate in this universe?

But authentically it's a box of illusion;
Learning to swim in the middle of an ocean
To an unknown journey;
With a collection of broken pieces,
But by assembling together, she becomes strong.

Do you really think life is full of green signals?
We see what's on the screen
But the truth is-
Everyone fights the battle for themselves;

Many a times red signals are on her way'
Regardless, she takes a little step audaciously
To break the stereotypes
Where she crosses shark as seal
However manifolds she is in a desert of dejection,
Which is surrounded by cactus
But somehow she survives

CHAPTER FOURTEEN

She's trying to find her life's direction

Lonely soul,
Drifting adieu of metaphors and hyperbole*
In the end, everyone turns yellow
Like autumnal leaves
She is like a golden fibre that needs to darn parts
It's alright to fill with misty - eyes, sometimes
Feeling barren and shattered from the core
Yet she can shed salty droplets in rainy nights
But it is too heavy to portray abstract in an art piece
As if she has lost her direction in the ocean fierce
But she wants to fly high like a kite.

CHAPTER FIFTEEN

Unstoppable

You may bruise her skin
But you cannot murder her thoughts
You may hurl her through arrows
But she is a seed, she will grow
She knows her shortcomings
Poetry has barely any limitations
Till her last breath, she will battle against wrongdoers
You may pull her down
But not to live in false vanity
You cannot stop her to shine less
She is a flame who burns and highlights
The darkness of ignorance
You may throw acid in her face
But you cannot stop to chase her passion
You may try to oppress her by showing superior to her
She's borne* to carry her wounds
Life lifted her with glorious things
She's not afraid for the whine*
Even if she will be physically impaired,
She will not resist growing.

CHAPTER SIXTEEN

You're a dot unless you connect lines

Keep walking
Till death embrace you
A traveler who lost his path, once
Stands in the epicenter of crowd
Experiences of dry ink, yellow pages
Doesn’t define you

CHAPTER SEVENTEEN

She is growing

Days are full of chaos,
Regardless of darkness with fireflies
Under the galaxy
Where she can inhale and breathe out freely
She no more wants a shoulder who can console her
Some changes lead us to maturity indeed.

CHAPTER EIGHTEEN

Ain't lonely

The pen is my drugs,
Each time it lightens the path of dusk,
The world is full of selfish people
I am not lonesome if I have a notepad.

CHAPTER NINETEEN

Perspective varies

It’s heartbreaking
When your partner doesn’t reciprocate
The way you love
You wait for him
To have a little cuddle
And a forehead kiss
Even not a gratitude speech
Both works 9 to 5
But he behaves he’s superior
Then why can’t he help in cooking too?
Isn’t he hungry?
Why is home science not a compulsory subject?

CHAPTER TWENTY

Behind the bars

Behind the bars,
Does she know what starry nights are like?
Behind the bars,
Does she know how streets look on rainy days?
She wears shackles
She's ungrateful as a human
Because she is void
She is scared to raise her voice
What if they dumped her under the soil
But she resembles herself with fireflies
One who burns self
To lighten the surrounding
Behind the bars,
Her dreams are chained
She wishes she could have wings to fly.

CHAPTER TWENTY-ONE

Fixing myself

Poetry flows in my veins like blood
Though I am stubborn, at times'
However, I have a passion to do
Not great, but small things with efforts
Although I am a slow learner
Yet I never back out amidst
Every now and then, I weave my broken parts
Carving into melodic phrases
Fixing myself with every frailty.

CHAPTER TWENTY-TWO

On the barren streets of life

I‘m not ludicrous*
I allow creating a mess
But often ends up with melting glaciers
Rising bricks of unloveliness
Relishing chromatic hues
Livin’ the blue vision
Walking on the thorns
Enabled to enhance my knowledge.

CHAPTER TWENTY-THREE

Do love can change people?

I never believed in the power of love
Because I was born into a family
That suppressed the color of skin and fluency of words
I witnessed the coercion*
Marks of iron to hide under layers of makeup
To serve all as they had bought me in dowry only to give service 24/7
It doesn't make any sense to them
How much I do to maintain the balance of the environment!
But at the end, they yell at my slightest mistake
They consider themselves as god and goddess
They doubted me in my upbringing.

CHAPTER TWENTY-FOUR

A blend into purple

Poems are mosaic* made of broken candelabra*
Verses filled with anxious metaphor
Remember nothing, but an amazing expression
To vent out every emotion at a time
Sometimes to walk away without any reason
Poets are nothing but a lost lover
Who admires sketch and words on a white canvas
To split ink of distinct hues
Sometimes to walk over those cracked pieces of glass
But the inner agony is heavier than the visible scratch
Poet bleed rosy
Poet blend into purple
Shrieking in the midnight, especially
And sometimes the dawn
Shine every day by rolling salty tears
Mosaic is created with a full teaspoon of dedication
With half spoon of memories
Pinch of loyalty
Higher amount of credits*
Less amount of withdrawal*.

CHAPTER TWENTY-FIVE

Regrets

Sometimes I regrets for my past
Sometimes I feel exhausted
Sometimes I am madly in love
Neither I can go back and erase it
Nor anyone will accept me for who I am
In fear of judgements, I lose myself
I have nothing to address as mine.

What am I?
A path finder?
Peeping from kaleidoscope of life's journey
Hanging with yesterday's lies
Hoping for tomorrow's burning candle
Disturbed, depressed, discomfort or to discover
Fear of body shaming, fear of critical comments
I lose myself in search of refined archetype.

Illuminated thoughts, twilight, under the cosmos
Feels like box with minute, malefic* witch
Distracted from the aims of my birth, my existence
Goodbyes to sincerity and great affection
Living outside a real life
Deeper the lines, carries abundance of failures

A lie to self is always a betrayal to oneself.

Everyday when I close my eyesight
Sometimes I feel this is last day to wave hands to the world
Sometimes I feel I live in a hallucinations
Building layers of poetic verse with sweet and sour experience
Walking like a wanderer
Watching like a eagle's prey
Sometimes I need to sit under a tree who give a little shade.

CHAPTER TWENTY-SIX

Why did I jot it down?

Why did I jot it down?
A talent to play with variant words
A talent to place letters in a right position
Artist lives the same life in a different way
A desire to make life vibrant
Not a writer, but a nib that speaks
Not a lyricist, but an instrument that keep-alive
Suicide, fake smile, gloom, speak less
Hustle, self-motivation, nomadic, disloyalties.

Why did I jot it down?
To speak ocean of wordage
That is suppressed in the traces of archaeological sites
Speaking with a pen is a reason to escape from the fantasy
Living with the same character daily is less possible
Drinking champagne, penning microtale, composing about deficiency
Enemies, circumstances, environment make us bravery
Dear ones treat us as guest
Just a wanderer, wandering for some peace.

Why did I jot it down?
At the age of twenty, motivational songwriter

Gulping sour episodes with a wide smile
Life, living with dead emotions, shooting words
Highlighting dark genres,
Sometimes queer, self - care, sometimes bowing down
Let us live or escape
But not to be a servant of own failure.

Why did I jot it down?
I hardly write non-fiction
I write not to achieve artificial name
I write as it gives me inner peace
I will be a mixture of mud and water
I am nothing after my burial,
I am not wearing a label of any brand or identity
My name is enough to express who I am
I am nothing just a gypsy.

CHAPTER TWENTY-SEVEN

Homecoming is depressing

Homecoming is depressing
Dowry is what they protest
But when it's their turn
It's not considered as dowry but as a gift
Can't we demand gifts?
They taught their children as-

//Man should depend on their wife for food,
Women should depend on their husband financially//

Instead of teaching, one must be financially independent and capable of doing individual works
For some, a home is a place of serenity
For a few, home is a dungeon
Where hardly they breathe and less suffocates.

At the age of twelve
Puberty knocks to each one of us
Around the world
Where in some parts, girls are not allowed to make friends with boys.

At the age of eighteen
She has been seen as a marriage product
There're many question-answer sessions
Where she shouldn't ask any questions in return
Her job is to give only answers
If she does, she is disobedient.

At the age of twenty-one
She's lucky if she has graduated
Her priority should be marriage.

At the age of twenty-five
After that, no good looking man will approach her
According to society, society comes afterward
If her parents fail to understand her wishes
If not them then who?
She is enough to stand for her!

At the age of 30
They mock her, as she fails to give birth to a child
Her in-law's behavior changes towards her, as she is a burden to them
They need to feed her but there's no fruit out of it.

At the age of thirty-five
She signed on divorce papers
As usual society satires at her state.

At the age of thirty-eight
She cleared state public service commission examination
Now her parents want her back home
But she refused to go

Even if they are her parents
But when they failed to stand in her weaker days
Why should she return to that place?

At the age of forty-two
She opened an orphanage
She has no child of her blood
But she gave a home to a couple of orphans.

Glossary

Tranquility - an untroubled state
Pisa - site of the famous leaning tower (Italy)
Imagery - imagination
Metaphor - a figure of speech in which an expression is used to refer to something that it does
not literally denote similarity
Symbolism - the use of symbols to represent ideas or qualities.
Sanguine - Confidently optimistic and cheerful
Serenity - absence of mental stress or anxiety
Carnal - sexual
corpse - the dead body of a human being
Audacious - fearless
hyperbole - presentation of something as more extreme than it really is
borne - move while holding up
whine - complain in an annoying manner,
Ludicrous - foolish
Coercion - the practice of persuading someone to do something by using force or threats
Mosaic - art consisting of a design made of small pieces of coloured stone or glass
Candelabra - branched candlestick
Credit - (compliment, hugs,...)
Withdrawal - (restrictions, ...)
malefic - evil

9 798885 914895

Printed by Libri Plureos GmbH in Hamburg, Germany